A Rainforest Habitat

Introducing Habitats

W9-AWD-035

Molly Aloian and Bobbie Kalman

Crabtree Publishing Company

www.crabtreebooks.com

Created by Bobbie Kalman

Dedicated by Samantha Crabtree
To Kingsley Bennett, the great adventurer who has traveled more of the world
from his mother's womb than most do in a lifetime.

Editor-in-Chief
Bobbie Kalman

Writing team
Molly Aloian
Bobbie Kalman

Substantive editor
Kathryn Smithyman

Editors
Michael Hodge
Kelley MacAulay

Design
Margaret Amy Salter
Samantha Crabtree
(cover and series logo)

Production coordinator
Heather Fitzpatrick

Photo research
Crystal Sikkens

Special thanks to
Jack Pickett and Karen Van Atte

Illustrations
Barbara Bedell: page 32 (middle)
Katherine Berti: pages 15, 20, 32 (top left)
Bonna Rouse: page 32 (top right)
Margaret Amy Salter: page 32 (bottom)
Tiffany Wybouw: page 26

Photographs
© Bauer, Erwin & Peggy/Animals Animals - Earth Scenes: page 22
BigStockPhoto.com: pages 4, 6, 13 (bottom), 17 (bottom right), 19 (bottom)
iStockphoto.com: pages 7, 11, 12, 13 (top), 14, 16 (top), 17 (top left), 20,
    32 (middle left and bottom)
© Francois Savigny/naturepl.com: page 21
Photo Researchers, Inc.: Alan Carey: page 10; Sam Fried: page 8; Art Wolfe: pages 25, 29
© Doug Perrine/SeaPics.com: pages 26-27
Visuals Unlimited: Theo Allofs: page 16 (bottom left); Henry Lehn: page 18;
    George Loun: page 30; Joe McDonald: page 23; Fritz Polking: page 31
Other images by Corel, Creatas, Digital Vision, and Photodisc

Library and Archives Canada Cataloguing in Publication

Aloian, Molly
    A rainforest habitat / Molly Aloian & Bobbie Kalman.
(Introducing habitats)
ISBN-13: 978-0-7787-2958-7 (bound)
ISBN-10: 0-7787-2958-3 (bound)
ISBN-13: 978-0-7787-2986-0 (pbk.)
ISBN-10: 0-7787-2986-9 (pbk.)
    1. Rain forest ecology--Juvenile literature. I. Kalman,
Bobbie, date. II. Title. III. Series.

QH541.5.R27A46 2006   j577.34   C2006-904090-7

Library of Congress Cataloging-in-Publication Data

Aloian, Molly.
    A rainforest habitat / Molly Aloian & Bobbie Kalman.
        p. cm. -- (Introducing habitats)
    ISBN-13: 978-0-7787-2958-7 (rlb)
    ISBN-10: 0-7787-2958-3 (rlb)
    ISBN-13: 978-0-7787-2986-0 (pb)
    ISBN-10: 0-7787-2986-9 (pb)
    1. Rain forest ecology--Juvenile literature.   I. Kalman, Bobbie.
II. Title.
QH541.5.R27A46 2006
577.34--dc22
                                                    2006018785

Crabtree Publishing Company

www.crabtreebooks.com   1-800-387-7650

Printed in Canada/112022/EF20220921

Copyright © **2012 CRABTREE PUBLISHING COMPANY**. All rights reserved. No part of this publication may be reproduced, stored in a retrieval system or be transmitted in any form or by any means, electronic, mechanical, photocopying, recording, or otherwise, without the prior written permission of Crabtree Publishing Company. Due to rights restrictions and copyright protection, contents in this ebook may vary from the published original. In Canada: We acknowledge the financial support of the Government of Canada through the Canada Book Fund for our publishing activities.

Published in Canada
Crabtree Publishing
616 Welland Ave.
St. Catharines, Ontario
L2M 5V6

Published in the United States
Crabtree Publishing
347 Fifth Ave
Suite 1402-145
New York, NY 10016

Published in the United Kingdom
Crabtree Publishing
Maritime House
Basin Road North, Hove
BN41 1WR

Published in Australia
Crabtree Publishing
Unit 3-5
Currumbin Court Capalaba
QLD 4157

Contents

What is a habitat?

A **habitat** is a place in nature.
Plants live in habitats. Animals
live in habitats, too. Some
animals make homes in habitats.

Living and non-living things

There are **living things** in habitats.
Plants and animals are living things.
There are also **non-living things**
in habitats. Rocks, water, and dirt
are non-living things.

Everything they need

Plants and animals need air, water, and food to stay alive. Plants and animals find the things they need in their habitats. This caiman needs water. It swims and finds food in the water.

Staying alive

This squirrel monkey lives
in a habitat. Everything the
monkey needs to stay alive
is in its habitat. The monkey
has found a piece of fruit to eat.

What is a rain forest?

A **rain forest** is a habitat. There are many trees in a rain forest. Rain forests are in parts of the world that get a lot of rain. Rain helps trees grow. Rainforest trees grow to be very tall.

The amazing Amazon

This book is about the Amazon rain forest. The Amazon rain forest is in South America. Many plants and animals live in this rain forest. This iguana lives in the Amazon rain forest.

Rainforest weather

The Amazon rain forest is near the **equator**. The equator is an imaginary line around the center of Earth. The weather near the equator is hot all year. The weather is hot in the Amazon rain forest. This baby ocelot is hot. It is cooling off in some shade.

Pouring rain!
It rains almost every day in the Amazon rain forest! When it rains, parts of the rain forest become covered in water. The bottoms of these trees are covered in water.

Rainforest plants

Many trees grow in the Amazon rain forest. Rainforest trees are very tall. Some are as tall as apartment buildings! Other plants grow in the Amazon rain forest, too. Some of these plants are bushes. Others are vines.

flower

Flowers and fruit

Many of the plants
in the Amazon rain
forest have flowers.
The flowers are colorful.
Some plants also have
fruit. Mango trees have
both flowers and fruit.

fruit

Making food

Living things need food to stay alive. Plants make their own food. They make food from sunlight, air, and water. Making food from sunlight, air, and water is called **photosynthesis**.

Taking it all in

A plant gets sunlight through its leaves. It also gets air through its leaves. A plant gets water through its roots. A plant uses sunlight, air, and water to make food.

Leaves take in sunlight.

Leaves take in air.

Roots take in water from soil.

15

Rainforest animals

blue morpho butterfly

These animals live in the Amazon rain forest. They are able to live in this hot, wet habitat. The animals know how to find food. They also know how to find homes.

coati

keel-billed toucan

Amazon river turtles

blue poison frogs

jaguar

golden-headed lion tamarin

Finding food

Animals must eat to stay alive. Some animals eat only plants. Animals that eat plants are called **herbivores**. This macaw is a herbivore. It eats nuts and seeds.

Eating animals

Other animals are **carnivores**. Carnivores eat animals. This jaguar is a carnivore. It eats fish, frogs, and turtles.

Eating both

Some animals are **omnivores**. Omnivores eat both plants and animals. This monkey is an omnivore. It eats fruit and insects.

Getting energy

sun

All living things need **energy**. They need energy to grow and to move. Energy comes from sunlight. Plants get energy from sunlight. Animals cannot get energy from sunlight. They get energy by eating other living things. A capybara is a herbivore. It gets energy by eating grass.

grass

capybara

Eating animals

Carnivores get energy by eating other animals. This puma is a carnivore. It gets energy by eating capybaras.

In the trees

Many rainforest animals live in trees.
Some animals swing from tree to tree.
This woolly monkey swings from
tree to tree. It uses its long arms and
strong hands to swing.

Flying high

Some rainforest animals fly. Birds and bats are animals that fly. They flap their strong wings. They fly from tree to tree looking for food. This short-tailed bat is flying around looking for food.

On the forest floor

Some rainforest animals live on the ground. The ground in the rain forest is called the **forest floor**. This millipede has many legs. It uses its legs to walk on the forest floor.

Life on the bottom

This Brazilian tapir lives on the forest floor. It rests under trees during the day. At night, it walks around looking for food to eat. The tapir eats fruits, leaves, stems, and other plant parts.

In water

A huge river flows through the Amazon rain forest. The river is called the Amazon River. Many animals live in this river. They find food in the river, too. Amazonian manatees and tucuxi dolphins live in the Amazon river. They are both good swimmers!

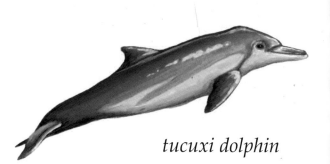

tucuxi dolphin

Staying safe

Rainforest animals must stay safe from the animals that hunt them. They stay safe in different ways. Some rainforest animals live high in the trees to stay safe. Animals that live on the forest floor cannot reach the animals in the trees. This sloth lives high in a tree.

Hard to see

These moths have brown bodies. Their bodies
are shaped like leaves. There are brown leaves
on the forest floor. The moths are safe because
they look like the leaves. Other animals may
not notice the moths on the forest floor.

Making homes

Some animals make homes in the Amazon rain forest. They stay safe inside their homes. These ants made a home under the ground. They are carrying small pieces of leaves into their home.

Nests in trees

Rainforest birds make homes called **nests**. They make nests in the trees. They use plant parts to make their nests. These jabiru storks made a nest in a tall tree.

Words to know and Index